Survey of Research in Sociology and Social Anthropology in North East India (1970-1990)

Nikhlesh Kumar

2026

Regency Publications

A Division of

Astral International Pvt. Ltd.

New Delhi – 110 002

First Published, 1999

Reprinted, 2026

ISBN: 978-81-86030-87-5 (Hardback)

Published by : **Regency Publications**
A Division of
Astral International Pvt. Ltd.
– ISO 9001:2015 Certified Company –
4736/23, Ansari Road, Darya Ganj
New Delhi-110 002
Ph. 011-43549197
E-mail: info@astralint.com
Website: www.astralint.com

Printed at : **Replika Press Pvt. Ltd.**

FOREWORD

The Advisory Committee of the NERC-ICSSR, Shillong at its meeting held on November 22, 1991 decided to sponsor the review of the literature on North-East India in the academic disciplines of Economics, Geography, History, Political Science, Sociology and Social Anthropology during the period 1970–1990. Consequently scholars in these fields were identified and the work was entrusted to them. Most of the scholars who were invited to review the literature in their subjects have either completed their work or are in the process of completing it soon. We are therefore, in a position now to publish these reviews one by one. The Review of Literature on North-East India in Political Science by Professor L.S. Gassah is the first publication in this series.

Review of published literature on North-East India in Sociology and Social Anthropology was entrusted to Dr. Nikhlesh Kumar of the Department of Sociology, North-Eastern Hill University, Shillong. Dr. Kumar has taught the subject for a number of years and has published a number of articles and has edited one book. He makes full use of his wide teaching and research experience in this review of literature in Sociology and Social Anthropology.

Sociology as an independent academic discipline has made considerable progress in India. In the north-eastern region, however, it is taught and studied only in a few institutions. The sociological and social anthropological studies in the region have, lately, attracted the attention of a large number of academics. It is heartening to note that the academics from other parts of the country are also now showing keen interest in the peoples and the cultures of this region.

A work of this kind requires the cooperation of a number of scholars in the field as well as adequate resources. North-East India is an extensive region having its own problems and difficulties. Keeping all these in view the review of literature was limited to publications in the English language alone. Dr. Kumar has tried to collect all the available publications in English in this work and has made it as complete and comprehensive as possible.

We take this opportunity to thank him for his painstaking work and for cooperating with the NERC-ICSSR, Shillong.

We are glad to offer this Review of Literature on North-East India in Sociology and Social Anthropology by Dr. Nikhlesh Kumar, the second publication in the series, to the general public and the students and scholars interested in the study of different aspects of the literature developed in these twin disciplines on North-East India during 1970–1990, not only within this region but also outside, and hope that it will be useful both to students and scholars alike.

Shillong
May, 1998

Jai Prakash Singh
Honorary Director
NERC-ICSSR

PREFACE

The North-Eastern Regional Centre of the Indian Council of Social Science Research (NERC-ICSSR) at Shillong commissioned this survey of sociological and social anthropological literature on the societies living in the north-eastern states of India. The task was confined to the review of the relevant literature produced between 1970–1990.

The vast amount of literature produced during these two decades lies in the libraries of the various institutions in the region. Under the constraints of the logistics we could cover the libraries in Shillong, Guwahati and Agartala. So rich were the collections that I decided to set aside the articles published in journals, many files of the seminar-proceedings, masters and research degree-level dissertations. I was consequently left with a large number of books, monographs and edited volumes.

My analysis reveals that most of the studies lack a comparative perspective and depth in the treatment of the subject. The authors of these studies have ignored rigour in their conceptual frameworks. There is very little literature on the non-tribal societies of the region. Above all, there is a great dearth of literature on inter-community and intra-community conflicts and the mechanisms of adjustments in the region. Despite of all the short comings the available literature has its own use-value for future researchers.

I would like to put on record my appreciation of the initiative taken by the NERC-ICSSR, Shillong in commissioning the study. I hope that this work will be found useful by those who are interested in carrying out research on the region. I wish to express my thanks to the NERC-ICSSR, Shillong for giving me opportunity of producing this work.

May 1998

Nikhlesh Kumar
Department of Sociology
North-Eastern Hill University
Shillong 793 014

CONTENTS

INTRODUCTION

Indian Council of Social Science Research (ICSSR), New Delhi, had published a series of survey reports in 1985 covering various aspects in the fields of sociology and social anthropology. The reports were based on the survey of literature produced during 1969–79. The eminent contributors to these volumes made comprehensive survey of literature produced in the country during the specified periods. In contrast to this the North-Eastern Regional Centre of the ICSSR (NERC-ICSSR) at Shillong commissioned the survey of literature in sociology and social anthropology covering a span of twenty years (1970–90) and restricted to societies of the north-eastern region of the country.

The term 'north-eastern region' is a politico-geographical term used for the states of Assam, Meghalaya, Nagaland, Arunachal Pradesh, Mizoram, Manipur, and Tripura. All these states touch the international boundaries of India with various countries. These states have come to acquire a strategic importance for the country and therefore enjoy a special consideration in the developmental plans of the country. The dominant populations living in these states, which claim themselves as traditionally indigenous, have had historical experiences quite different from the people living in other parts of India — particularly those living on the Indian mainland.

Out of the seven states mentioned above four states (Meghalaya, Arunachal Pradesh, Nagaland, and Mizoram) are the hill states while the remaining three states have societies differentiated on the basis of those living on the hills and those living in the plains. Even in each of the four hill-states we have different societies speaking different languages which are now in the process of evolving a common minimum identity as members of the state they inhabit and as citizens of the nation (India) of which their state is an integral part.

Traditionally, indigenous societies of the north-eastern region claim that they had migrated to these parts of the region from either the Mongolian heartland of Central Asia or from some parts of the South-East Asia. It is in this sense that these societies do not claim an aboriginal status in this region. These migrations took place at different times and through different routes. In the absence of any historical records and other scientific evidences it is difficult to say whether the structures and cultures of these societies as witnessed now could help us trace their links to locate their places of origin. It is also difficult to say whether such issues in the present day context will have any scientific value for investigation! Moreover, the societies living on the hills acquired a written language only recently and any accounts available about them are furnished by those who came from other societies and areas and interacted with them.

The earlier contacts with the outside world of these peoples, so to speak, were with the Turks in the first instance and with the Mughals subsequently who invaded the regions now in India from the north-western direction and managed to reach Bengal.

Contact of these societies with the outside increased with the coming of British who wanted to exploit the vast natural resources of the region. Harassed by the stiff opposition from the natives the East India Company used its superior military power to contain the armed resistances. The Company entered into various types of treaties with the local chiefs. Administrative means were devised to regulate the contact of the people living in the region, particularly on the hills, with the people living in other parts of India. Selected groups of people from the eastern part of Bengal (now Bangladesh) were sent to this region to run the administration of the Company in the earlier years and later that of the British Crown. Of course, certain changes were effected in the lifestyle of these people by introducing modern education, modern medicine, modern economy, a new religion in the form of Christianity, and the Roman script amongst those people who did not have a script of their own.

All these efforts had a lasting impact on the people of this region in many ways. But to do all these things it was found necessary to make a study of these societies. Monographs were prepared by the British civil and military officials on the basis of observations (though not scientific) and information gathered by them during the tenure of their work in different parts of the region. These monographs cannot be accepted as scientific studies but these do provide information helpful in designing systematic research on the various aspects of these societies.

Systematic studies were conducted later on by trained anthropologists in the Anthropological Survey of India. Till India became independent Calcutta University was the only major centre of learning nearest to the region. But after independence a university was opened at Guwahati (1948) which subsequently started a department of anthropology. Department of sociology came up for the first time in the region in mid-1960s with the establishment of Dibrugarh University in Assam. These departments of anthropology and sociology focussed their research activities on the societies in the north-eastern region unlike their counterparts in other universities in the country with perhaps the only exceptions of the Universities of Delhi and Ranchi. The department of sociology in the University of Delhi has a special programme by the name of the North-East Hill Area programme under which students hailing from the north-eastern region are admitted for training at the postgraduate and doctoral levels. Department of anthropology of the same university also gives special attention to training the students coming from this region. In addition to the teaching and research departments in the Indian universities the state governments in the region have their research departments to conduct research on the societies living in their respective states. Mention may be made especially of the Research Department of the Government of Arunachal Pradesh.

The decade of 1970 has a special significance in the context of our discussion at present. In 1973, a central university by the name of the North-Eastern Hill University (NEHU) was established at Shillong. This university started a combined department of sociology and anthropology in 1976. Around the same time the ICSSR opened its regional centre at Shillong referred earlier as the NERC-ICSSR and attached it with NEHU. This regional centre gave a boost to the research activities by funding seminars and research projects. Besides this some intellectuals in the city of Shillong, with the help of others in the region, established a research-oriented forum by the name of the North-Eastern Council for Social Science Research (NEICSSR). The NEICSSR provides a platform to the scholars and other intellectuals in the north-eastern region to come together and discuss various contemporary issues related with the societies of the region. In a way we can say that the decade of 1970 saw the sudden spurt in the research activities and production of scientific literature as well as increase in the academic interaction and exchange of research experiences in a directed and coordinated manner.

This brief historical sketch can be concluded with the remark that the sudden turn of events in the second-half of the decade of 1970 on the front of contemporary research and exchange of ideas showed positive results in the next decade when we see the vast literature describing various aspects of the north-eastern societies and issues thrown by the rapid currents of change in the region.

The vast literature produced in these twenty years lies in the libraries of various institutions in the region. Given the difficulties in visiting these libraries personally letters were issued seeking help from the scholars in various states of the region. Requests were sent to them to suggest names of persons who could assist in this endeavour. Much time was wasted in this fruitless persuasion and ultimately some assistants were appointed from amongst the students of NEHU who did their best to scan the major libraries in Shillong, Guwahati, and Agartala. Dibrugarh had to be unfortunately left out finally since no local assistance was available from there.

This survey report is arranged state-wise indicating the literature produced on the societies in each state of the region. In spite of the fact that the bibliography on the subject could not be made exhaustive it can be said with confidence that the coverage of the literature is so extensive as to show the trend of research in sociology and social anthropology during 1970–1990.

I

MEGHALAYA

The Khasi Milieu edited by Mawrie and Miri (1981) throws light on the tribal religion of the Khasi society. The authors stress the point that in spite of a non-literary tradition the Khasi tribal religion is quite rich in ideas. The various articles try to explain the influence of Khasi religion on different aspects of the life of the people; the relationship between man and nature; or the concept of God and the relationship between Man and God.

Nalini Natrajan in her book *The Missionary Among the Khasis* (1977) describes the role and work of the Christian missionaries among the Khasi of Meghalaya. Comparing the pre-Christian Khasi society with the Christianised society after the arrival of the Christian missionaries she has tried to explain the impact of the missionaries on the Khasi society. She used the technique of structured questionnaire and interview guide for data collection to present a picture of the contemporary Khasi society.

Sebastian Karotemprel's book *Albizuri among the Lyngams* (1985) presents an historical account of the activities of the Catholic mission in the western part of the Khasi Hills. This particular part is largely inhabited by the Lyngams — a lesser known community of the Khasi. Most of the work on the Khasi tribe relates to the people living on the uplands. Fr. Karotemprel's work tries to expose this community to the academic world by giving a detailed ethnographic account of the Lyngams. While dealing with the pioneering missionary activities of Fr. Albizuri this work throws ample light on the culture and various institutions of the Lyngam Khasi society.

We came across three monographs on the ethnography of the Khasi society. *The Khasis* by S. Barkataki (1977) followed the style of a classic by the same title written by Col. P.R.T. Gurdon in the first decade of this century. Barkataki has devoted almost half of the book to describe various Khasi folklores while in the other half considerable attention is focused on the tribal laws, customs, and religious beliefs of the Khasi society.

The Khasi Canvas by J.N. Choudhury (1978) is more comprehensive in its coverage. It discusses the geography, flora and fauna of the Khasi Hills as a part of its description of the land and the people. Besides describing the kinship structure of the society it also informs about the occupational practices and material aspects of the culture of the people. The last section of the book deals with the political history of the society by comparing the changes during the British period and after independence of India.

P.R.G. Mathur's book *Khasi of Meghalaya — Study in Tribalism and Religion* (1979) deals with issues relating to religion, tribalism, and nationalism in the context of the Khasi society. The author has tried to analyse the changes coming about in the Khasi society as a result of the changes experienced in the religious system and the traditional political system. Interestingly, the book has a chapter on the Muslim Khasi — unlike other similar works which deal only with the role of the Christian missionaries.

P.K. Das Gupta in his work entitled the *Life and Culture of Matrilineal Tribe of Meghalaya* (1984) has dealt with the aspects of material culture, economic, social, political, and belief systems of the Khasi living in the War area of the Khasi society. This work provides information on these people living on the southern slopes of the Khasi Hills bordering Bangladesh.

Tribal Institutions of Meghalaya, edited by S.K. Chattopadhyay (1985), and *Assortment from Tribal Research Institute, Meghalaya* by R. Kostan Roy (1978) both deal with the political institution in the Khasi society. The former work is a collection of articles by different scholars on various aspects of political administration, justice, landownership, religious beliefs and practices, and kinship structure of the Khasi, Jaintia, and Garo societies. The latter work deals with the history of *Hima* Nongkhlaw (Nongkhlaw tribal state), analysis of kinship terminologies, and some beliefs.

M.K. Sukumaran Nair in his book *Tribal Economy in Transition* (1987) presents an empirical study of agriculture in Khasi Hills. He describes the land tenure system, organisation of labour; and processes of production and consumption. He also discusses the transition from shifting to settled agriculture. Though this study is based on the methods of economic analysis yet it is a useful work for the students of sociology and social anthropology.

Shillong — the capital city of Meghalaya — has been a capital city since its inception. In the course of its over-a-century old history it has attained the status of a cosmopolitan city with its own culture. We found three books devoted to the study of this city. *Cultural Profile of Shillong* edited by B.B. Goswami (1979) is a collection of articles read earlier in a seminar on the same theme. The articles are divided into three sections: Shillong as an Urban Centre; Cultural Core and Diversities; and Emerging Cultural Features of Shillong. The articles discuss the geography, history, demography of the city; the role of educational institutions, and the Christian missionaries; the inter-ethnic conflicts. Then there are some articles dealing with the growth of Khasi literature, pop music groups, game of archery, etc. The overall thrust of the articles was on identifying the problems in the inter-ethnic adjustment and the impact of this cosmopolitan life on the Khasi society.

Shillong 1971–81, edited by B. Pakem (1984), is a collection of papers presented in a symposium on the same theme organised in 1981 by the North-East Indian Council for Social Science Research, Shillong. Divided into five sections, this book discusses various aspects of this cosmopolitan capital town. The contributors have described the administrative, political, economic, cultural, educational profile of the city.

There is absence of an exclusively sociological work in the area of Urban Sociology on any urban area of the state. J.P. Singh's work *Urban Land Use Planning in Hill Areas* (1980) is a work in the field of Urban Geography. We have included this work here because it describes certain aspects of the empirical reality which would also be of use to the studies in the field of Urban Sociology — at least in the generation of some meaningful hypotheses. In the context of the geography and history of the city of Shillong this work throws light on the demographic structure of the population; the patterns of residential, commercial, and other forms of landuse. Describing the urban front of Shillong the author also discusses issues in urban planning.

Hamlet Bareh's book *Meghalaya* (1974) is a general work on the state of Meghalaya. He discusses about the culture of the three major tribes (Khasi, Jaintia, and Garo) of the state. It traces the history of the creation of Meghalaya and the changes in the three tribal societies after the creation of this state.

A Tribe in Transition — The Jaintias of Meghalaya is a monograph on the Jaintia tribe written by H.L. Deb Roy (1981). It describes in details the Jaintia kinship and marriage systems, religious system, cosmology, mythology. The treatment of the transition aspect in society is insufficient. Similarly the work ignores emphasis on the political and economic institutions of the Jaintia society.

The Jaintias by S.K. Chattopadhayaya (1988) is a work more comprehensive in approach than the work of Deb Roy (1981) mentioned above. Chattopadhayaya deals with the kinship, marriage, religion, economy, political structure of the Jaintias. He has even presented a comparison between the Garo and Jaintia political systems.

The Origin and Early History of the Khasi-Synteng People by Namita Catherine Shadap-Sen (1981) has more emphasis on the Jaintia tribe than the Khasi tribe. The work is based on archaeological and historical evidences gathered from secondary sources than on empirical evidences based on primary sources. Yet the work may be of interest to the students of sociology and social anthropology as it provides information on social, religious, political, and economic institutions of these societies in the past.

The People of Meghalaya — Study on the People and their Religio-cultural Life by Capt. B.S. Rana (1989) discusses in general terms certain aspects about the Khasi, the Jaintia, and the Garo tribes of Meghalaya: the geographical location, physical characteristics of the hills predominantly inhabited by these tribes, kinship organisation, marriage practices, food consumed, eating and drinking habits, architecture of their houses, religious beliefs and practices, etc. The work does not provide any meaningful insight into the life-styles of the these tribes.

D.N. Majumdar and B. Datta-Ray co-authored a book, *Tribal Occupational Mobility* (1984). This is an empirical study of the occupational structure of the Khasi, Pnar, and Garo populations living in the cities of Shillong, Jowai, and Tura respectively. The authors wanted to find out the changes in the occupation from agriculture to others as a result of the growth of these three urban centres in the state. Moreover, the authors also tried to examine the correlation between occupational mobility and social mobility; and inter-generational occupational mobility.

A Century of Government and Politics in North-East India, Vol. II (Meghalaya: 1874–1983) by V. Venkata Rao, B. Pakem, and N. Hazarika is a study based on various historical sources and official documents of the government. The book presents in a chronological manner the governance and the administration in the North-East from the British period onwards and throws light on the conditions for the formation of the state of Meghalaya. The book may provide a general secondary source reference to a scholar interested in the area of political sociology.

M.C. Goswami and D.N. Majumdar edited book *Social Institutions of the Garo of Meghalaya — An Analytical Study* (1972) is an empirical work on the kinship and marriage systems; customary laws in the Garo society. It also analyses the change in the Garo society from communal ownership of land to the private ownership of land. The authors have also touched upon the issues related to the position of women in the Garo society.

J.B. Bhattacharjee's work, *The Garos and the English* (1978) is the work of an historian which gives an insight into the changes experienced by the Garo society after coming in contact with the British particularly between 1765 to 1874. The book focusses attention mainly on the administrative development, moral and material progress of the Garos. It attempts to assess the impact of the British rule on the political, social, and economic life of the Garos.

A Study of Culture Changes in two Garo villages of Meghalaya by D.N. Majumdar (1980) is a study of the two villages practising different modes of cultivation. The village still following the traditional shifting cultivation showed less changes in the life-style and social institutions as compared to the village which had switched over to the settled mode of cultivation. The later village had also shown emergence of other forms of economic activities.

History and Culture of the Garos by Milton S. Sangma (1981) is another work by an historian. The book throws light on the traditional, political and judicial systems in the Garo society; revenue administration; and religion. It can serve as a secondary source material to a student of sociology and social anthropology.

The Garos in Transition by P.C. Kar (1982) is a comprehensive account of the Garo economic institution written by an economist with the perspective of economic anthropology. It is an empirical work based on data collected from the village Darengri. In his analysis, the author has tried to delineate the exogenous and the endogenous forces effecting change in the socio-economic life of the Garos.

Garo Hills — Land and the People edited by L.S. Gassah (1984) is a collection of articles contributed by scholars from the disciplines of Sciences, Social Sciences, Humanities, and Environmental Sciences. These contributions are helpful in getting a general view of the Garo society from various perspectives.

Garo Customary Laws and Practices — A Sociological Study by Julius Marak (1986) deals at length with the Garo social institutions, laws, and customs. It also tries to explain the effect of Christianity on the life of the Garos. The author maintains that though the spread of Christianity did bring about changes in the economic condition of the people yet their customary laws remained unaffected.

The Tribes of Meghalaya — A Bibliography by Sipra Sen (1985) is a good reference work for any student who wishes to do research on the societies in the state of Meghalaya. It presents brief introduction of the Khasi, the Jaintia, the Garo, and the Hajong tribes of Meghalaya. The bibliographical references in an unannotated form are given tribewise and drawn from various sources. A total of 1597 references are listed in the book.

Impact of the West on Khasis and Jaintias — A Survey of Political, Economic and Social Change by P.N. Dutta (1982) presents an exhaustive account of the British policy towards the Khasis and Jaintias. It tries to explain the political, economic, and social changes in these societies since their earlier contact with the British. The author has tried to examine in details the various aspects of the British policy and the response of these tribes to the British policies.

Social and State Formation in Khasi Jaintia Hills by Soumen Sen (1985) has attempted to study the history, culture, social and political institutions of these two tribes by analysing their myths, legends, rituals, folktales, and folksongs.

P.R. Kyndiah in his book, *Meghalaya — Yesterday and Today* (1990) describes the folklore and culture of the various tribes of the state. Tracing the history of the emergence of the state the author has attempted to place the present-day state in the background of the past of its major inhabiting tribes.

II

NAGALAND

India — The Land and People (Nagaland) by Prakash Singh (1972) is a book on the developments in Nagaland after the independence of India. The thrust of the work is on the aspirations of the Nagas, the politico-economic changes in the Naga societies, and the role of the foreign powers in augmenting the insurgency activities in the state of Nagaland.

Social and Cultural Life of Nagas — The Tangkhul Nagas by M. Horam (1977) is a monograph on the Tangkhul Naga society. It is an empirical study on the structure and culture of the Tangkhul Naga tribe. The author also touches upon the issues of underdevelopment of this society and offers some suggestions for its development.

Milada Ganguli's book, *A Pilgrimage to the Nagas* is an English translation of the original work in the Czech language. The work is descriptive in nature and is a combination of the historical account of various Naga tribes and the author's observation during her travel to various parts of the Naga Hills. Giving a vivid account of the organisation and culture of various Naga tribes the author brings out differences amongst them and attempts to explain the difficulties in the assimilation of these tribes in the Indian mainstream.

Nagaland File — A Question of Human Rights by Luingam Luithui and Nandita Haksar (1984) is a collection of documents relating to the manifestoes of various Naga underground groups, various agreements signed between the Indian government and different Naga groups; special legal provisions applicable to Nagaland; various reports on the violation of democratic rights of the Nagas. The book divided into various sections has very informative sectional introductions.

Tribes of Nagaland by Sipra Sen (1987) is a comprehensive unannotated bibliography of about 2000 published and unpublished materials on Nagaland. It also gives a brief description of the State of Nagaland; its districts; and short ethnographic accounts of some of the Naga tribes.

The World of Nagas by Murkot Ramunny (1988) is a descriptive account, based upon secondary source materials, of the Nagas after the Indian independence.

Nagas: Old Ways New Trends by M. Horam (1988) is an insider's account of the effects of the process of modernization on the Nagas. The book is based upon the personal experiences and impressions of the author who belongs to one of the tribes of the Nagas. The author has attempted to re-examine the Naga society and culture in the wake of tremendous changes going on in the society.

III

MIZORAM

The Land Where the Bamboo Flowers by J.D. Baveja (1970) is a monograph on the Mizo society. It describes the kinship and marriage systems, religion, political and economic systems of the Mizos. The author has highlighted the processes of political and economic development in the society. He has also dealt at length with the factors that led to the Mizo rebellion of 1966. The work based on the earlier writings of the British administrators and the author's own experiences is quite useful in getting a simple overview of the Mizo society.

The Mizos — A Study in Racial Personality by Lal Biak Thanga (1978) is a work based upon secondary source materials. It describes the early history of the Mizos and traces the migration of the society from their place of origin to the Mizo Hills. It also describes their traditional religion, customs, folklores, folktales, folkmusic. The author also describes the changes in the Mizo society after the advent of the British and after the independence of India.

Lushai Customs and Ceremonies by B.J. Dev and D.K. Lahiri (1983) describes the traditional customs of the Lushai tribe amongst the Mizos regarding kinship, marriage, death and certain aspects of religion. The authors also discuss the impact of modernising forces on their traditional social order and politico-economic development. They also discuss the traditional and contemporary statuses of the Lushai chiefs.

Kuki — Life and Lore (Vol. I) by Tarun Goswami (1985) is a descriptive account of the traditional life and culture of the

Kuki tribe. With the help of the folklores, folksongs, and folkmusic the author has attempted to describe various aspects of the Kuki life e.g., activities during childbirth, marriage ceremonies, building of a new village, rituals before hunting expeditions, etc.

Leadership Among the Mizos — an Emerging Dimension by P.K. Bandyopadhyay (1985) discusses the emergence of new leaders in the Mizo society as a result of Christianity and their contact with the British administrators. This new leadership has been viewed as a dimension of change in the traditional political system where the leadership has rested with the village chiefs. As a study in the field of political sociology this work is quite useful for researchers.

IV

TRIPURA

Tripura: Its History and Culture by Omesh Saigal (1978) is divided into three parts. In the first part he has described the physical location of Tripura and the history of the people. In the second part he has discussed about the various ethnic groups inhabiting this state: the Bodos, the Kuki-Chin tribes, the Tripuris, some other tribes, and the non-tribal Bengali population. In the third part the author has dealt with the practice of jhum cultivation, and has recorded some folksongs and folktales.

Treatise on Traditional Institutions of the Tripuri Community by Debapriya Debbarman (1983) is a monograph on the Tripuris who constitute the largest tribal group in Tripura. The work deals with the kinship, marriage, and religious systems of Tripuris. It describes the traditional village administration, folkmedicine, folksongs, folklore, etc. In the end the author also discusses the impact of the forces of modernisation on the life of this tribe.

The Koloi in the Light of People's History by P.N. Bhattacharjee (1983, English edition) is a monograph on the Koloi community belonging to the Tripuri community. The author describes the marriage system, religion, traditional administrative system, and folk literature of the Koloi.

The Riangs of Tripura by J. Gan Choudhuri (1983) is a work on the second largest tribe (Riang) of Tripura. This empirical work discusses the social organization, economic activities, religious beliefs and practices, traditional political organisation of the Riangs. It also describes the natural environment in which they live and the history of their migration to the Tripura Hills. The author has also dealt with the effects of changes in the occupational structure from hunting to the emergence of the white collar jobs.

Kamilini Ghosh (1984) in her book *Tribal Insurrection in Tripura* tries to explain the causes of insurgency in Tripura. She argues that the process of modernisation was linked with insurgency. She maintains that the developmental processes were bringing a crisis of identity amongst the tribals. She has also examined the success of various policies and programmes of the state government to contain the feeling of deprivation and alienation amongst the tribals.

The Jamatia of Tripura by P.N. Bhattacharjee (1984) is an empirical study of some Jamatia villages of Tripura. The monograph gives a detailed account of the kinship and marriage systems, political system, and the religious system of this tribe.

Tribes of Tripura — A Historical Survey edited by S.K. Saha (1986) is a collection of articles by various scholars covering a wide range of topics of general interest.

A Political History of Tripura by R.M. Sarma (1986) covers the pre-Manikya period, Manikya dynasty, the Muslim hegemony, and the British paramountcy. This work of an historian can serve as a background material even for a student of sociology.

Tripura Administration — The Era of Modernisation by Banikanta Bhattacharyya (1986) is an extensive work tracing the development of administration in Tripura from the ancient period till the seventh decade of the present century. Students of political sociology may find this work useful while designing their research.

Socio-economic Survey of the Noatia Tribes by S.B. Saha (1986) is an empirical work dealing with the demographic structure, the agrarian structure, the economic status of the families, etc. of the villages studied by him.

Tripura by S.N. Guha Thakurta (1986) presents a brief ethnographic account of the people of Tripura. The author has also discussed various problems faced by the society due to the sudden increase in the population in the 1950s, its peculiar geographical location, lack of infrastructural facilities, unemployment etc.

Tribal Insurgency in Tripura by S.B. Bhattacharjee (1989) deals with the physical features of Tripura; the demographic, social, and cultural life of the people; the economic and political organisation. It also deals with the chronological development of tribal movements, and features of insurgency.

A Corpus of Tripura by J. Gan-Choudhuri (1990) consists of articles written on varied aspects of the life of people in Tripura. It describes certain communities of Tripura, the hunting and fishing crafts, the condition of Tripuri women, the Tripuri folktales, etc.

V

MANIPUR

Meitei Villages (Imphal East Block) Manipur: Rural Development Plan, is a project report prepared by the Association of Voluntary Agencies for Rural Development, New Delhi (1975). The report is based upon an extensive survey of the geo-physical features of the area; land use; agriculture and agricultural practices, and allied occupations; market organisation; socio-economic infrastructure; types of industry; irrigation facilities; etc. Based on the information on all these factors the report suggests a plan for the development of the agricultural and non-agricultural sectors.

Integrated Area Development Plan for West District, Manipur by Waheeduddin Khan and K.S. Ramesh (1976) is an empirical study of the Nungba Sub-Division and the West District of Manipur. In this monograph the authors have presented nodal points for infrastructural and social facilities and have also tried to delineate their zones of influence. On the basis of their projections they have suggested plans for the agricultural development in the region.

The Religion of Manipur by S.N. Parratt (1980) is an empirical study of the belief system and rituals in the Manipuri society. With the help of a survey of traditional religion she could argue that it had only superficial similarity with the Burmese religion. It had its own gods and priests. On coming in contact with the Hinduism the society adopted the Chaitanya school of Vaishnavism. The book presents a well-argued account of the religious and cultural practices of the Manipuris.

The Anals of Manipur by Capt. Rajendra Singh (1981) is an empirical study of the Anals — a lesser known tribe of Manipur. In this monograph the author has presented an account of the origin, migration, village organisation and defence, political organisation, customary laws, religion and religious practices, etc. of the Anals. The author has also tried to study the impact of the outside world on their traditional life-style.

Manipur — Maid of the Mountains by R. Constantine (1981) is a monograph on Manipur. The author while giving an account of the Meiteis in Manipur valley tries to analyse the causes of the political violence in Manipur.

Social Change in Manipur edited by B.K. Ahluwalia and Shashi Ahluwalia (1984) is a collection of articles by various scholars on Manipuri language, martial arts, literature, and performing arts. In the appendices the book gives an account of the origin and religion of Manipuris.

Anal: A Transborder Tribe of Manipur by G. Kabui (1985) is an empirical study of two Anal villages. The monograph describes the location of Anal inhabitation in the Manipur South district, their origin, migration, physical characteristics, kinship and marriage systems; and political, religious, and economic systems. The author has also described the interrelationship between the two villages.

Manipur Tribal Scene — Studies in Society and Change by Rajat Kanti Das (1985) focuses attention on the interrelationship between the tribal societies on the hills of Manipur and the non-tribal Meitei society living in the valley. The author emphasises on the problems of identity faced by the tribal people in the wake of the forces of change affecting their societies.

Proceedings of the Symposium on Purum (Chote) Revisited edited by B.K. Das Gupta *et al* (1985) is a collection of articles by various scholars on different aspects of the Chote tribe written on the basis of largely demographic and cultural anthropological data. One of the main issues was to consider the reasons for the change in its name by the tribe from Purum to Chote. Another issue was the impact of forces of change on the identity and cohesiveness of the tribe. It is quite a comprehensive work to be consulted by those who will be interested in further studying this tribe.

Socio-Economic Development in Tribal Area of Manipur by S.A. Ansari (1986) is an empirical study of the Nungsai Chiru village. In this monograph the author has argued that in spite of its limited resources this hilly village has benefitted by its contact with the Meiteis in the valley. The author suggests that this agriculture-based village should improve its quality of agriculture for its socioeconomic development.

Manipur: Religion, Culture, and Society by C.S. Panchani (1987) claims to deal with the issues relating to the society, religion, art, and culture of the people of Manipur in the context of their geography and history. The author also describes the temples in Manipur and the Christian and Muslim institutions.

Manipur — Culture and Politics by Bimal J. Dev and Dilip K. Lahiri (1987) gives an account of the history, culture, and politics of Manipur. The authors have also attempted to explain the causes of insugency in Manipur.

Manipur — Past and Present (*Vol. I*) by N. Sanajaoba (1988) is a collection of articles on the multi-faceted aspects of the civilisation of Manipur. The volume provides a detailed historical and economic account of Manipur.

Tribal Social Structure — A Study of the Maring Society of Manipur by R.K. Das (1988) is an empirical study of the Maring society of Manipur. In this exhaustive monograph the author has described the society mainly in terms of its kinship structure. The author has also examined the interrelationship of this society with its neighbouring society known as Tarao. The author maintains that various forces of change have left the structural characteristics of the society unaltered.

VI

ARUNACHAL PRADESH

The Tai Khamtis edited by Lila Gogoi (1971) is a collection of articles on the Tai Khamti tribe of Arunachal Pradesh by various scholars. In this comprehensive work the editor has selected such writings which throw light on the history, ethnology, language, culture, myths, trade practices of the Khamtis. The editor claims that this is the first ever comprehensive compilation in the English language on the Tai Khamti society.

A Comparative Study of Adi Religion by J.N. Chowdhury (1971) is based on published materials and reports. The author has attempted to explain Adi religious ideas and practices by drawing a comparison with the religious beliefs and practices as found in the Vedas, Puranas, and popular mythology of the Hindus. The author maintains that the Adi religion possesses all the ingredients of a high religion.

Arunachal Panorama — A Study in Profile by J.N. Chowdhury (1973) is a compilation of essays on different tribes of Arunachal Pradesh. The book presents short ethnographic accounts of these tribes inhabiting the different districts of the state. In the end one chapter is devoted to the agricultural practices and the land ownership pattern in the state.

Among the Wanchos by L.R.N. Srivastava (1973) is an empirical study based on data collected from 38 Wancho villages over a period of two years. In this monograph the author has described the geographical setting of their villages; their social, political, economic, and religious institutions.

The Hill Miri by B.B. Pandey (1974) is an empirical study of this little known tribe of Arunachal Pradesh. In this monograph the author has tried to touch upon almost all the aspects of the Miri society but for their kinship and marriage systems. However, their religious beliefs and practices have been more highlighted.

The Tangams by T.K. Bhattacharjee (1975) is a monograph on a small society known by the name of Tangams who are living in relative isolation. The author has described aspects of their kinship, marriage, occupation, religious beliefs and practices, customary laws. The author has also described certain artifacts used by them. He has also highlighted the efforts of the government in developing the economy of these people and in maintaining their cultural distinctiveness.

The Singphos and their Religion by T.K.M. Baruah (1977) is an empirical study of the Singpho tribe. The monograph is divided into two parts. The first part consisting of three chapters gives a brief introduction of the social organisation and culture of these people. The second part consisting of eight chapters is the more substantial part of the book where the author has dealt with the religious beliefs, rituals, artifacts used for the rituals, magical practices, etc.

The Noctes by Parul Dutta (1978) is an empirical study of the Nocte tribe of Arunachal Pradesh. The monograph gives a description of the ecology of the Nocte habitation, their origin and migration legends, their physical characteristics, etc. It gives detailed exposition of their domestic life; and social, political, and religious institutions.

The Ramos of Arunachal — A Socio-Cultural Study by M.M. Dhasmana (1979) is an empirical study of the Ramo tribe. It describes their pattern of settlements, social institutions, economic institutions, political institutions, and religious institutions. The work also touches upon the relationship of Ramos with their neighbouring tribes.

The Pailibos by K. Kumar (1979) is an empirical study describing in details the topography, climate, flora and fauna, demographic features of the Pailibo tribe. It also describes their trade-routes. The monograph gives details of various institutions of the society, culture, artifacts, dress styles, etc.

The author has also touched upon briefly on the effect of the processes of modernisation on their life.

Lower Siang People by Paramanand Lal & Biman Kumar Das Gupta (1979) is an empirical study of the tribes living in the Lower Siang area of Arunachal Pradesh. The book is divided into two parts. The six chapters in Part I give a description of the tribal villages, settlement patterns, and house-types, agricultural practices and other aspects of their economic activities, material artifacts and food habits. The four chapters in Part II describe their social, political, and religious oganisations, and their life-cycle. The authors found that though the ecological variations in the area run from north to south the cultural variations run from east to west. The different groups living adjacent to each other maintain their cultural differences.

The Land of Mon by Neeru Nanda (1982) is an ethnographic account of the Monpa tribe inhabiting the Tawang area of Arunachal Pradesh. The book describes the kinship and marriage system of the Monpas, their village organisation, and village economy. A major part of the work is devoted to the religious beliefs of this Buddhist community where the author noticed the existence of features of pre-Buddhist practices as well in their rituals.

Highlanders of Arunachal Pradesh — Anthropological Research in North-East India by Christoph von Fürer-Haimendorf (1982) is an ethnographic account of the various tribes of Arunachal Pradesh. In the background of their traditional societal characteristics and practices the author has tried to explain changes experienced by some of the major tribes (with particular reference to the Apatani tribe) in the socio-economic sphere.

The Sulungs by R.K. Deuri (1982) is an empirical study of the Sulung tribe of Arunachal Pradesh. In this monograph the author has presented a detailed descriptive account of the various institutions of this society. The author has commented that it was too early then to discern the impact of modernisation on this society.

The Idus of Mathun and Dri Valley by T.K. Bhattacharjee (1983) is an empirical study of this tribe living in the remote parts of Arunachal Pradesh. The author has described the various institutions of this tribe along with their customary practices relating to disputes and conflict resolution.

Tribal Songs of North-East India by A.B. Kar Choudhury (1984) is a monograph on the folksongs and folkmusic of the Khamti and Mishmi tribes of Arunachal Pradesh. The author has tried to explain the folkmusic in the context of the lifestyles of these people and the position of women in these tribal societies.

Tribes of Arunachal Pradesh by P.T. Nair (1985) gives an overview of over a dozen tribes. Special attention has been paid on the institutions of youth dormitories, marriage, and slavery. The author has also touched upon their earlier contacts with the British. He has argued that the British policy of keeping these tribes secluded from other parts of India had helped these tribal groups in preserving their cultures.

The Wealth of Arunachal Pradesh by S.D. Jha (1985) is a comparative study of the geo-economic and the socio-economic variables of development of the various tribes of Arunachal Pradesh. The author has also focussed on the traditional as well as the emerging sectoral variables of economic development.

Arunachal Pradesh and the Tribes — Select Bibliography by Sipra Sen (1986) is a very comprehensive unannotated bibliography on the various tribes and the state as a whole. The list of references is preceded by a description of the districts and a brief description of the tribes. The references in the book cover the materials produced between 1932 and 1985.

Socio-Economic and Demographic Dimensions of Arunachal Pradesh by S.D. Jha (1988) covers a vast range of issues concerning the organisation of agriculture and related economic activities, problems of industrialisation; problems of unemployment, demographic features, etc. The book is a collection of articles on diverse topics.

Arunachal Pradesh: Religion, Culture and Society by C.S. Panchani (1989) focusses attention on the religion and culture of the tribes of Arunachal Pradesh. He introduces the tribes, in this book, in their historical and geographical contexts. The main attempt of the author is to show that the religions of these tribes are linked with the pre-historic Siwalik culture of the western Himalayas. The author has also tried to link their religion with the great epic literature of the Hindus.

The Tribal Culture and History of Arunachal Pradesh by J.N. Choudhury (1990) has viewed the tribal culture in the historical perspective — beginning from the pre-historic times through the British rule to many years after the independence of India. The author observes that the British policy of 'exclusion' of these areas from other parts of British India had kept these tribal societies in isolation. But after the independence these societies have shown tremendous progress in various fields. The author contends that their administrative and socio-economic development is spectacular.

The Monpas of Arunachal Pradesh by D.K. Duarah (1990) is an empirical study of the physical characteristics of the Monpa boys. The data were collected from different villages and educational institutions. The author has also compared the physical growth pattern of the Monpa boys with other Mongoloid tribes of the North-eastern region, viz., the Khamti, the Ahom and the Rabha. He found that the Monpa boys were shorter in height and lighter in weight as compared to their counterparts in the other tribes mentioned above.

Social Organisation of the Minyongs by L.R.N. Srivastava (1990) is an empirical study of the Minyong tribe. The author has described the family and marriage systems; and their death and eschatological beliefs.

Aspects of Culture and Customs of Arunachal Pradesh edited by P.C. Dutta and D.K. Duarah (1990) is a compilation of 30 articles by the officers of the Research Department of the Government of Arunachal Pradesh. These articles were earlier published in the bi-annual journal *Resarun* of the department between 1977 and 1987. Most of the articles based upon empirical data are descriptive in nature.

The Singphos by Parul Dutta (1990) is an empirical study of the socio-cultural life of the Singpho tribe. The author has dealt with their kinship and marriage systems, life-cycle rituals, dormitories, festivals and dances.

The Wanchos by Parul Dutta (1990) is an empirical study of the Wancho tribe. The monograph deals exhaustively with the ecological features of their habitat, the village settings, their economic activities, political life, socio-cultural life;

religion and religious ceremonies. The author has also touched upon certain aspects of change affecting the Wancho society over the years.

Arunachal Pradesh — From Frontier Tracts to Union Territory by J.N. Choudhury (1983) is a monograph on the history of Arunachal Pradesh from earlier times till its formation as the Union Territory. Given the various difficulties faced due to its topography the author has thrown light on the various plans introduced for its development. This work can serve the research students as a good introductory reference.

VII

ASSAM

Tribal Folktales of Assam (Hills) compiled by S.N. Barkataki (1970) contains the folktales of the Hill tribes of the erstwhile composite state of Assam. In all 129 folktales are compiled in this volume which reveal the traditions, beliefs, and customs of these peoples.

United Mikir and North Cachar Hills by B.N. Bordoloi (1972) is a descriptive account of the various tribes inhabiting the hills of Assam and their economic activities. It serves a general introductory work on this part of the state of Assam.

Tea Garden Labourers of Assam by S.S. Harlalka (1975) is a study of the social and economic conditions of the tea garden labourers. The study focusses attention on the problems of the labourers and their dependents engaged in the tea gardens of Assam.

The Dimasa Kacharis of Assam by B.N. Bordoloi (1976) is an empirical study of the various aspects of life and culture of the Dimasa Kachari society inhabiting the North Cachar Hills district of Assam. This monograph provides an account of the traditions and customs of these people.

The Dibongiyas by P.C. Saikia (1976) is a descriptive study of the Dibongiyas who are considered as a priestly community. This monograph describes the social organisation of this community, and the changes coming about in their social life and the religious practices.

Tai-Ahom: Religion and Customs by Padmesawar Gogoi (1976) is a collection of ten research papers written by the author under the UGC's scheme of "Utilization of the Services of the Retired Teachers." These articles bring to light the lesser known aspects of Assamese culture i.e., the religious beliefs, rituals, and various customs of the Tai-Ahoms. The author has also tried to assess the impact of Hinduism on the original Tai-Ahom culture.

The Economy of Karbi-Anglong by Pradip Kumar Gogoi (1978) is a statistical analysis of the socio-economic structure of Karbi-Anglong. The author has analysed the data available from 1951 and presented a comprehensive analysis which will be quite useful for other researchers.

Among the Dimasa of Assam — An Ethnographic Study by Dipali G. Danda (1978) is an empirical study of the Dimasa society and its culture. This monograph presents a comprehensive ethnographic account of the Dimasa society.

Social Relations in an Ahom Village by Indira Barua (1978) is an empirical study of a village community. Describing the social, religious, economic, and political life in the village, the author has tried to show that all these aspects of the village life were experiencing the impact of change. But there was also a tendency to revive the traditional religious system.

Tea Garden Labourers of North-East India — A Multi-Dimensional Study on the Adivasis of the Tea Gardens of North-East India, edited by Sebastian Karotemprea and B. Datta-Ray (1979) is a collection of almost three dozen research articles covering the social, economic, and political situation of the tribal population engaged in the north-eastern tea gardens as labourers.

Assam and the Assamese Mind edited by N. Saikia (1980) is a collection of articles by the intellectuals of Assam. It gives an overview of the history and heritage, values and virtues, and hopes and fears of the Assamese. The editor hopes that the volume will create an awareness of Assam and her people in the minds of the readers.

The Tai of Assam and Ancient Tai Ritual, Vol. I, by B.J. Terwiel (1980) is a comprehensive account of the ancient Tai life-cycle rituals. The author has made an empirical assessment of the extent to which the ancient rituals have been retained by the Assam Tais.

Caste Status and Power—Social Stratification in Assam by S.K. Chauhan (1980) is an empirical study of the system of social stratification in the Assamese rural society. The author contends that in the wake of the modern political forces the rural power structure is getting more differentiated and dispersed.

Tribes of Assam Plains by M.M. Choudhury (1980) is a brief descriptive account of seven tribes living in the plains of Assam. The author has presented their short historical background, and described their traditions, culture, and features of village economy.

Tradition and Style by Maheswar Neog (1981) is a collection of 15 articles by the author. These articles based on secondary source literature cover various aspects of Assamese culture ranging from ancient past to the present. Special attention has been paid to the evolution of performing arts in Assam.

The Tai of Assam and Ancient Tai Ritual, Vol. II by B.J. Terwiel (1981) presents a detailed ethnographic description of four distinct Tai groups: the Ahom, the Khamyang, the Phakeng, and the Khamti. These four groups have been compared with the Tai groups outside Assam. The author has also focussed his attention on the sacrifices and time-reckoning system among the Tai societies.

N.C. Pegu (1981) in his work, *The Mishings of the Brahmaputra Valley*, presents a descriptive account of the life and culture of the Mishings. Based on secondary source materials this book attempts to project a composite image of the Mishings.

Chomangkan — The Death Ceremony Performed by the Karbis by B.N. Bordoloi (1982) is a monograph giving a vivid description of the death rituals performed by the Karbis. The author has attempted to highlight the socio-religious significance of the death rituals.

The Tai Phakes of Assam by G.C. Sharma Thakur (1982) is an ethnographic account of this Buddhist population of Upper Assam. He has described their economic activities, religious practices, folk beliefs, concepts of law and justice, etc. The author has also tried to highlight how this small population has managed to retain their traditions and culture.

Demographic Trends in Assam (1921–71) by T.K. Chaudhuri (1982) is based on an analysis of demographic data of 50 years.

He has tried to explain the population trends in Assam in comparison to other states of India.

Politics of Alienation in Assam by Bhawani Singh (1984) highlights the Bengali-Assamese linguistics dispute, and the sense of alienation in the Assamese society. The author has tried to analyse the ethnic and linguistic tensions in Assam and has tried to suggest some possible solutions to reduce such tensions.

The Assamese by Audrey Cantlie (1984) is an empirical study of an Assamese village. The author has described the kinship and marriage systems, the religious system, the caste system in its historical perspective, and certain religious sects in the Assamese society. The author has also analysed the impact of the new reform movements of the 1930s on the traditional institutions of the Assamese society.

Cosmology of Caste and Social Mobility in Assam by Bimal J. Dev and Dilip K. Lahiri (1984) is a description of various caste groups in the Assamese society. The authors have presented the description in comparison to the caste groups and inter-caste relations in the mainland India. The authors have also highlighted the lack of rigidity in the inter-caste relations in Assam as compared to the situation in other parts of the country.

The Ex-Tea Garden Labour Population in Assam by Umananda Phukan (1984) is an intensive socio-economic investigation of the people known popularly as the ex-tea garden labourers. Tracing the history of their migration to Assam from outside Assam in the second half of the 19th century the author has attempted to analyse the problems of their rehabilitation in the villages of Assam.

Spatial Structure of Urban Influence in the Neighbouring Areas of Gauhati City by Jayasree Borah (1985) attempts to analyse the patterns of urban-induced effects of Gauhati on its neighbouring areas. She has tried to understand these effects in terms of the demographic and socio-economic features of the areas around Gauhati. This analytical work can be useful to the students of urban sociology.

Modern Assamese Life and Culture edited by Birendranath Datta and Amarjyoti Choudhury (1985) is a collection of articles on the life and culture of the Assamese people by eminent scholars of Assam.

The Mataks and their Kingdom — Castes and Tribes of Assam by S. Dutta (1985) is an attempt to understand the history and culture of the Mataks, an aboriginal people of Assam. The author has described the composition of the Matak community, their socio-economic life, religious beliefs and practices. The author has also described the Matak challenge to the Ahom and the subsequent establishment of the Matak kingdom. The author has described the contemporary situation as well of the Matak community.

The Lalungs (Tiwas) by G.C. Sharma Thakur (1985) is an empirical study of the Lalung society. In this monograph the author gives an account of the social institution, religious beliefs and practices, festivals, aspects of material culture of the Lalung society. The author has also analysed the effects of the developmental efforts of the government on the life of these people.

The Semsa and their Habitat by Dipali G. Danda and Sanchita Ghatak (1985) is an ethnographic account of the Semsa tribe of North Cachar Hills of Assam. This area of Assam is inhabited by various communities living side-by-side with their neighbours in their respective ecological niches. The study highlights the strains on the society due to their continued practice of shifting cultivation and increase in population. The authors have brought out the interesting fact that in spite of several constraints the Semsa have continued to live in their traditional village for over two centuries.

Population Trends in the Brahmaputra Valley by Homeswar Goswami (1985) seeks to analyse and explain the trends, fluctuations, and patterns of population and its principle components in an historical perspective in the Brahmaputra valley of Assam during the period 1881–1931. The author has laid more emphasis on the determinants rather than the consequences of population trends and fluctuations.

Sociology of the Karbis by Tanmay Bhattacharjee (1986) is an empirical study of the Karbis. The monograph was prepared for the benefit of the administrators. The author has described the origin; social, economic, political, and religious systems of the Karbi society. The author has also highlighted the controversy that had emerged on the name of the society.

A Glimpse of the Scheduled Castes and their Socio-Economic Development in Assam by Bhakta Das (1986) highlights the problems faced by the scheduled castes in Assam and the attitude of the higher castes towards the lower castes. The author describes the origin of the scheduled castes in Assam and views them in the wider context of the Indian caste system. The author has discussed the various administrative measures to uplift the status of these underprivileged castes.

The People of Assam by B.M. Das (1987) is a physical anthropological study of the Assamese population.

Medieval Assamese Society (1228–1826) by Sarbeswar Rajguru (1988) is a comprehensive account of the social, economic, political, and religious institutions of the Assamese society during the medieval period. It also deals with the development of Assamese literature and spread of education. The work is based on the material drawn from historical sources.

Bohag Bihu of Assam and Bihu Songs by P.D. Goswami (1988) describes in details one of the most important festival in Assam—the Bohag Bihu. The book contains more than three hundred folksongs connected with the Bihu festival.

A Socio-Economic and Cultural History of Medieval Assam (A.D. 1200–1800) by Satyendranath Sarma (1989) attempts to describe the socio-economic and cultural life in Assam during the medieval period. The author consulted various chronicles in the form of Buranjis, Rajavamsavalis, the Sattra Vamsavalis, etc.

Social History of Assam by M.L. Bose (1989) describes the pre-British history of Assam, formation of Assam province during the British period, demographic and cultural profile of Assam and the emergence of Assamese ethnic identity and social tensions in the state of Assam. The author also touches upon the effects of administrative developmental measures on the Assamese society.

Dimensions of Tribal Movements in India — A Study of Udayachal in Assam Valley by Madan C. Paul (1989) presents various aspects of the tribal movement known popularly as the Udayachal movement. The author argues that the contradictions introduced by the unequal socio-political forces in the tribal social system during the British colonial period and their consolidation in the post-independence period are perceived as a challenge by the tribals to their existence. The author has called for an urgent need of a radical transformation in the socio-economic system to remove disparities.

The Lalungs (*Tiwas*) by A.K. Baruah (1989) is a monograph on the Lalungs who largely reside in the Nowgong district of Assam. Based on primary data the author has described the kinship and marriage, economic, religious, and social institutions of this society.

Spotlight on Assam by S.K. Das (1989) is a secondry source-based work on the problems of immigration and demographic transformation of Assam. The author has tried to analyse the causes of problems faced by the people of Assam in the wake of continued influx of people from across the international border.

M. Kar (1990) in his book, *Muslims in Assam Politics* provides an indepth analysis of the Assam politics with special reference to the Muslims who constitute about one-third of the population of the state. On the basis of various official documents and other historical materials the study also traces the bases of conflict between the Assamese and the Bengalese in Assam.

Social and Economic Change in Assam — Middle Class Hegemony by Manorama Sharma (1990) is a work in the field of history. Yet it has a certain merit for a student of sociology. The author has examined the social roots of the middle class and has also tried to conceptualise the category *middle class* in the context of the Assamese society. Her analysis is based on the socio-economic changes in Assam during 1860–1910. She has termed this as the period of the emergence and growth of middle class.

VIII

GENERAL

Socio-Economic Research in Tribal Areas edited by P.C. Goswami (1971) is a collection of articles grouped in three sections: (i) social factors affecting economic development; (ii) problems of field investigation in tribal areas; (iii) village study as a tool of socio-economic research in tribal areas. All the papers have the developmental problems in the tribal areas as their focus.

Contemporary Anthropological Research in North-East India edited by B.M. Das (1974) is the Vol. III of the Bulletin of the Department of Anthropology, Dibrugarh University. The 27 articles here were presented in a symposium organized by the department. Almost all the articles are based upon researches conducted in the discipline of physical anthropology.

A Century of Tribal Politics in North-East India (1874–1974) by V. Venkata Rao (1976) is divided into three parts: Political Developments; District Councils; and State Politics. The book deals with the traditional tribal political systems, the effects of the British administration, and the formation of governments under the modern democratic political system of the country. It offers a good politico-historical account to the students of political sociology.

Religion and Culture of North-Eastern India by Raghuvir Sinha (1977) deals mainly with the religious philosophy, beliefs, and rituals in the North-Eastern Region. It is quite interesting to note here that the author speaks of the 'North-

Eastern Religion' as a type with its own philosophy and ritual ceremonies.

Human Sacrifice and Head-Hunting in North-Eastern India by Bikash Chandra Gohain (1977) is a study of the practice of Human Sacrifice and Head Hunting amongst the various societies of Manipur, Tripura, Assam, and the hill states which were earlier part of the composite state of Assam.

Castes, Tribes and Culture of India: Assam by K.P. Bahadur (1977) is a brief descriptive account of the Nagas, the Khasis, the Garos, the Mikirs, the Kacharis, the Santhals, and the Meiteis. The description mainly centres around the origin and habitat, general appearance, domestic life, religion, superstitions, and folklore of these societies.

Social and Economic Profile of North-East India edited by B. Datta-Ray (1978) is a collection of articles presented in a seminar on the 'Problems of Development of the North-East India.' The papers are classified around four themes: (i) profile of north-east Indian economy; (ii) levels of economy and the market; (iii) cultural perspectives; and (iv) prospects of integrated development.

Tribal Economy of North-Eastern Region edited by T. Mathew (1980) is a collection of papers presented in a seminar of the same theme. The focus of the contributors was on the problems faced by tribal economies of the region and the possible ways of solving these problems.

Glimpses of Tribal Life in North-East India by J.K. Bose (1980) is an empirical account of the structure and culture of some of the tribes of the north-eastern region. The main thrust of the work is on the kinship and marriage systems of the tribes.

Religion and Society of North-East India edited by Sujata Miri (1980) is a collection of articles contributed in a seminar at the North-Eastern Hill University, Shillong. The major thrust of the papers is on the plurality of religions co-existing with each other. Some papers deal with specific tribal religions, role of myth, spread of Christianity, and the concept of religious conversion.

Eastern Himalayas: A Study on Anthropology and Tribalism edited by T.C. Sharma and D.N. Majumdar (1980) is a collection of articles on ethnographical, archaeological, and cultural profiles of North-East India. The book also gives an outline of anthropological studies and research in the north-eastern region.

The Burning Caldron of North-East India by G.S. Ghurye (1980) deals with the problems of adjustment of the north-eastern tribes within the larger political system of India. The author contends that these societies were not a part of the socio-political mainstream of India until about a century ago. The British also followed a policy of isolation and thus hampered the process of interaction with the wider Indian society. The author argues that only a very high degree of political wisdom could bring peace and prosperity in the region.

Linguistic Situation in North-East India, edited by Mrinal Miri (1982) is a collection of papers read in a seminar on the same theme. Discussing the issues of development of the region the scholars highlighted the problems of inter-ethnic communication, linguistic identity, and the growth of ethnic consciousness on the basis of linguistic affiliation in post-independence period of India.

New Horizons of North-East by J.D. Baveja (1982) brings out the cultural diversity in the north-eastern region. He has tried to highlight the peculiar problems of various tribal communities in the region. In the end the author presents a comparison between the tribe's of north-east and north-west frontiers of India.

Essays on the Folklore and Culture of North-Eastern India by P.D. Goswami (1982) is a collection of folklores of various tribal and non-tribal communities of the region. It is, however, difficult to identify any thematic scheme behind the choice of various folklores in this work.

Social Tension in North-East India (Colloquium) edited by J.B. Bhattacharjee (1982) is a collection of articles contributed by various scholars in a colloquium on the same theme. The dozen-and-a-half articles discuss inter-ethnic tensions in Assam, Meghalaya, and the region as a whole. The contributors touch upon the issues of assimilation, influx of Nepalese and Bangladeshis, and the problems of inter-ethnic maladjustment.

Report of the Seminar on Tribal Situation in North-East India by National Institute of Public Cooperation and Child Development (1982) is a collection of articles by various scholars. The main thrust of various articles is the development of the tribals of this region. The scholars have tried to present an assessment of the developmental programmes and the response of the tribal societies to these programmes.

Human Resources of North-Eastern India by J.P. Singh (1982) is a study of all the seven states of the region from the perspective of regional economies. The author argues that the planning for human resource development has to be linked with the economic development measures. He has emphazied on the importance of local environment in the planning for the region.

The Emergence and Role of Middle Class in North-East India edited by B. Datta-Ray (1983) is a collection of eighteen articles covering most of the states in the region. The main thrust is on the changes that had come about in the village economy in most of the societies of the region and the consequent changes in the traditional leadership pattern. The emergence of a middle class in some of the tribal societies was indicative of the change in the leadership.

The Tribes of North-East India edited by S. Karotemprel (1984) is a collection of articles contributed by various scholars. The articles collectively bring out various facets of the cultures of different tribes of north-east India.

Towards Poverty Alleviation Programmes in Nagaland and Manipur by B.K. Roy Burman (1984) is an appraisal of the poverty alleviation programmes in the two neighbouring states of Nagaland and Manipur with reference to the provisions in the Sixth Five Year Plan of India. The author expresses disagreement with the National Committee on Development of Backward Areas recommendation of individualisation of communal ownership for the sake of 'progress'.

North-East Region Seminar on Problems and Prospects of Development edited by B.L. Abbi (1984) contains 26 articles contributed by the participants in the seminar. The book is divided into three parts. Part I consists of introductory papers on the perspective of the seminar. Part II contains articles dealing with the demographic transformation, economic development, and social tensions in the north-eastern region. Of the six papers in this part three papers were specifically on the situation in Assam. Part III has 26 papers devoted to the theme on 'social and cultural diversity and quest for national integration.' Here also about eight papers deal with the Assam agitation on foreigners' influx. Rest of the papers deal with the issues of cultural pluralism and related issues in the context of the region.

Electoral Politics in North-East India by S.K. Chaube (1985) is presented by the author as a companion volume to his earlier *Hill Politics in North-East India* (1973) where he had described the processes of reorganisation of the north-eastern states. In the present volume, based on the data from the Sixth Lok Sabha Elections (1977) the author analyses the features of the electoral politics in this region.

Focus on Folklore of North-East India edited by Birendranath Dutta (1985) is a collection of essays on the various folklores popular in the region.

Planning in North-East India, edited by K. Alam (1985) is a collection of papers presented in a seminar on the same theme. The various articles make a critical study of diverse aspectsof developmental planning in the region. The articles taken together focused attention on the following themes: (i) national and regional planning processes; (ii) social dimensions of planning; (iii) levels of planning; (iv) review and projection of growth in north-east India; (v) North-Eastern Council and regional planning; and (vi) strategies for long-term plan development.

The North East: Roots of Insurgency by P. Roy Choudhury (1986) is a monograph on the problems of insurgency in the north-eastern region. The author argues that the roots of insurgency lie in the designs of the imperialist powers who had systematically sown the seeds of discontent in the minds of the tribal communities of the region.

Land Use Pattern in North-East India edited by B.B. Dutta (1986) is a collection of papers presented in a seminar on 'Land in North-East India'. The contributors dwell at length on the types of land and the various land use patterns in the region. The focus of the contributors was also towards the formulation of a future policy of land use in the region.

Tribal Life of North-Eastern India by S.T. Das (1986) consisting of 15 chapters can be divided into two sections. The first section consisting of 11 chapters gives a general account of the geography, economic practices, religious beliefs and aspects of material culture of the region; the second section consisting of the remaining four chapters gives a brief ethnographic account of the Zumi Nagas, the Mikirs, the Kacharis, and some ethnic groups of Manipur.

The Pattern and Problems of Population in North-East India edited by B. Datta-Ray (1986) is a collection of 30 papers read earlier in a seminar on the same theme. Out of these there are 12 papers devoted exclusively to the studies on different parts of Assam. The papers in this volume deal with general demographic analysis of population, migration, growth in urban population, human resource development and unemployment, etc.

Social and Economic Development in North-East India edited by Shashi Ahluwalia (1986) is a collection of articles dealing with developmental issues concerning the region. The various articles deal individually with the development of agriculture, manpower, transport, energy, tourism, etc. Role of the North-Eastern Council has also been discussed.

Crime Perspective in North-East India edited by B. Datta-Ray, D.N. Majumdar, and D. Doley (1986) is a study based on the analysis of data obtained mainly from the prison records. The objective of this study was to find out social and economic parameters of crime in northeast India. The study also attempted to find out the adjustment problems faced by the convicts after their release from the prison. The study had concentrated mainly on the situations in Assam and Meghalaya.

Art and Culture of North-East India by L.P. Vidyarthi (1986) deals with the demography, ethnicity, history, changes in the practice of jhumming. It also deals with art and crafts, and cultural change in the north-eastern region.

North-East India — A.D. 2000 edited by B. Datta-Ray (1987) is a collection of papers presented in a seminar on 'North-East India A.D. 2000: Perspective for Futurology'. The various scholars, with a futuristic perspective, examine the basic issues of ecology, population, physical resources, scientific and technological applications, planning management, cultural resources, and institutional framework in the context of the north-east India. Taking stock of the progress made by the societies of the north-east this work attempts to project the picture of these societies in A.D. 2000.

Life Styles: Indian Tribes (Locational Practice), Vol. I, by S.T. Das (1987) deals with various tribes of the region. Based on secondary source material this monograph attempts to explain the distinctive characterising features of tribes. The author has included only those tribes which show marks of influence in their culture due to their interaction with the plains people. The author maintains that the various reform measures have created conflicts in the way of life of these societies.

Demographic Profile of North-East India by S.C. Srivastava (1987) is an analysis of the demographic data on various north-eastern states. The author claims that his exhaustive treatment of the data on various aspects of the north-eastern population will be useful for the planners and administrators.

Economic and Social Change in North-East by Habung Payeng (1988) focusses attention on the economic and political changes in some tribal groups of Arunachal Pradesh.

Economic Development of the North-Eastern Region edited by D. Bharali (1988) is a collection of about three dozen articles read in a seminar on the impact of the Five-Year Plans on the socio-economic growth of the North-Eastern Region. The papers deal mainly with the development of infrastructure, resources, industries, rural areas, commercial activities, banking, etc. in the region.

North-Eastern Economy—Problems and Prospects by A.K. Agarwal (1988) is a monograph based on secondary source materials. In the background of varying problems in planning for the development of the region the author attempts to examine the various issues involving the economic development of the region. The author has also suggested approaches and remedial measures to deal with the economic problems of the region.

Ethnic Identity, Ethnicity and Social Stratification in North-East India by N.K. Das (1989) is an empirical study attempting to analyse the factors of ethnic conflicts in the north-eastern region in the context of the ethno-historical processes. He also examines the processes of state formation in various tribes of the region.

Rural Development in North-East India edited by P.D. Saikia and U. Phukan (1989) is a collection of papers presented in a seminar. The papers deal with the problems of rural development and assessment of the various rural development programmes.

Sequences of Development in North-East India edited by J.B. Bhattacharjee (1989) is a collection of articles presented in a seminar on the same theme. The articles touch upon the various aspects of rural development, developmental programmes, planning, social change, processes of modernisation, etc. While many articles deal with the north-eastern scenario in general there are some articles dealing with specific areas of the region or specific issues, e.g., education, employment, etc.

Tribal Identity and Tension in North-East India by B. Datta-Ray (1989) is a monograph dealing with the dynamics of tribal identity in the region and the problems of inter-ethnic adjustments, regional stability, and socio-economic development.

Nationality, Ethicity, and Cultural Identity in North-East India edited by B. Pakem (1990) is a collection of papers presented in a seminar on the same theme. The various contributors argue that the questions of nationality, ethnicity, and cultural identity have assumed greater importance in view of the urgent need for the overall development of the region.

Roots of Ethnic Conflict (Nationality Question in North-East India) by Sajal Nag (1990) is a study based on the secondary source materials. The author has tried to analyse the Assamese society during the British colonial period. He has attempted to explain how changes came about in the Assamese society with the advent of British capitalism. He argued that with the further development of Assamese nationality came the conflict with the 'established and advanced nationality' of the Bengalese living in Assam.

Tribal Demography and Development in North-East India edited by Ashish Bose, Tiplut Nongbri, and Nikhlesh Kumar (1990) is a collection of 20 articles read in a symposium by the same name. The papers are organised under the following sub-themes: Perspectives and Issues in Development; Population Patterns, Occupational Structures; and Nutrition, Health and Education.

Nationality, Ethnicity and Cultural Identity in North-East India edited by B. Pakem (1990) is a collection of 30 articles presented in a seminar earlier. The book has some articles under a general section dealing with the issues of nation-building, ethnicity, nationality, etc. The rest of the articles relate to such issues in the context of each of the seven states of the region.

Social and Political Institutions of the Hill People of North-East India edited by Jayant Sarkar & B. Datta-Ray (1990) is a collection of 25 articles. The articles besides describing these institutions in different societies of the region also try to present the changes coming about in these institutions in the recent times.

Tribal Customary Laws of North-East India by Shibani Roy and S.H.M. Rizvi (1990) presents an inventory of the tribal customary laws of some of the major tribes of the region. The authors highlight the effect of the British administration on the customary laws of the tribal societies in the region. The customary laws have traditionally remained uncodified over generations. With the introduction of literacy in recent times and the attempt at codifying these laws the authors point towards the tendencies of misrepresenting the laws in order to exploit the natural resources to wrongful advantage by vested interests.

IX

SEMINAR PROCEEDINGS

Seminar on Youth Problems and Movements was organised by the Department of Sociology and Anthropology, NEHU, at Shillong, in 1978. The twelve articles read in this seminar focussed on the problems of youth in various societies and also cities of the region.

Seminar on the Status of Women in Tribal Cultures of Meghalaya was organised by the North-Eastern Regional Centre of the Indian Council of Social Science Research (NERC-ICSSR), Shillong, in 1988. The five contributors to the seminar described the traditional situation relating to the status of women in the Khasi, the Jaintia, and the Garo societies. The papers also discussed the changes in the traditional family situation due to the effects of Christianity, education, means of communication, employment in non-agricultural sectors, etc.

Seminar on the Status of Women in Tribal Societies of Mizoram was organised in Aizawl in 1988. The eight contributors discussed the role of women in the economic development of the state, in church, in social control; the effect of education on the status of women; etc. According to the contributors, women were considered as the backbone of the society and enjoyed a status equal to that of the men.

Seminar on the Status of Women in Non-Tribal Societies of Assam was organised by the Department of History, Dibrugarh University in 1988. In all 15 papers were read in the seminar. The papers were written on the following themes:

(i) general status of women; (ii) economic status of women: women, society, economy and culture; (iii) women, religion, and science; (iv) women in administration and politics; (v) women and violence; (vi) legal status of women; (vii) women and health care.

Seminar on the Status of Women in Naga Societies was sponsored by the NERC-ICSSR and held at Shillong in 1988. A total of 7 papers were presented in the seminar. The contributors argued that the level of female education was the indicator of the status of women in any society. They pointed out that introduction of Christianity and formal education had enhanced the status of women in many Naga tribes but there was a need for further improvement of their status.

Seminar on the Status of Women in Barak Valley was organised by the North-Eastern Institute of Anthropological Research, Silchar, in 1988. The total of ten contributors to the seminar discussed the status of women belonging to different communities living in the Barak Valley of Assam.

Proceedings of the Seminar on Sociology of Resource Use with Special Reference to Mizoram relate to the seminar organised by the Lunglei Government College, Lunglei, Mizoram, in 1990. The main objective of the seminar was to focus attention on the current social movements and changes in the context of the resources used for development. In all 11 scholars presented their papers. Most of the contributors laid stress on the development of economy and the development of human resource in the state.

CONCLUDING REMARKS

Though the author of this report has not made any claims of conducting an exhaustive survey of the literature yet the 195 entries annotated above do give a fairly good view of the trend of research in sociology and social anthropology in the region during the period under consideration.

A cursory glance at the state-wise breakup of literature will show that Assam had the maximum number (42) of entries; followed by 29 entries under Meghalaya and 27 entries under Arunachal Pradesh. Manipur and Tripura each had less than 20 entries while Nagaland and Mizoram had less than 10 entries each. There were 48 entries under the general category. This category included works which had a collection of articles on different societies of the region.

The number of empirical studies was less. The studies lack rigour both in theory and methodology. There is also an absence of empirical studies with a comparative perspective.

The societies in the north-eastern region of India are marked with linguistic diversity. Even in the states like Arunachal Pradesh and Nagaland with large numbers of tribes we come across a variety of languages. Different tribes use link-languages to communicate with each other and a mere knowledge of these link-languages does not always facilitate the field work. With the increase in the number of tribal students going for higher education it is hoped that more empirical studies will come up in near future and the existing literature will help in the formulation of good hypotheses.

I could identify the following areas in the literature surveyed by me: Tribal Ethnography; Institutions in Tribal Societies; Status of the Tribal Customary Laws; Tribal Belief Systems; Agricultural Practices and Land Tenure Systems; Ethnic Unrest and Protest Movements; Status of Women; Change, Development and Impact of various Developmental Schemes introduced by the Government.

The trend shows that the majority of the works could be broadly reclassified as those concerned with (i) the structural and cultural aspects of the societies; and (ii) the problems faced by the societies due to both the developmental measures and the lack of development of these societies.

BIBLIOGRAPHY

Abbi, B.L., *North-East Region Seminar on Problems and Prospects of Development*, Chandigarh: Centre for Research in Rural and Industrial Development, 1984.

Agarwal, A.K., *North-East Economy—Problems and Prospects*, Delhi: Mittal Publications, 1988.

Ahluwalia, S. (ed.), *Social and Economic Development in North-East India*, Delhi: Gian Publishing House, 1986.

Ahluwalia, B.K. & Shashi Ahluwalia (eds.), *Social Change in Manipur*, Delhi: Cultural Publishing House, 1984.

Alam, K. (ed.), *Planning in North-East India*. Guwahati: Omsons Publications, 1985.

Ansari, S.A., *Socio-Economic Development in Tribal Areas of Manipur*, Delhi: B.R. Publishing Corp., 1986.

Association of Voluntary Agencies for Rural Development, *Meitei Villages (Imphal East Block), Manipur*, New Delhi: Association of Voluntary Agencies for Rural Development, 1975.

Bahadur, K.P., *Caste, Tribe and Culture of India: Assam*, Delhi: Ess Ess Publications, 1977.

Bandyopadhyay, P.K., *Leadership Among the Mizos—An Emerging Dimension*, Delhi: B.R. Publishing Corp., 1985.

Bareh, H., *Meghalaya*, Shillong: North-East India News & Features Service, 1974.

Barkakati, S., *The Khasis*, Pathsala (Assam): A.P. Choudhury & Bani Prakash, 1977.

Barkakati, S.N., *Tribal Folk-Tales of Assam*. Gauhati: Publications Board, Assam, 1970.

Barua, Indira, *Social Relations in an Ahom Village*, New Delhi: Sterling Publishers Pvt. Ltd., 1978.

Baruah, A.K., *The Lalungs (Tiwas)*, Guwahati: Tribal Research Institute, 1989.

Baruah, T.K.M., *The Singphos and their Religion*, Shillong: DIPR, Govt. of Arunachal Pradesh, 1977.

Baveja, J.D., *New Horizons of North-East*, Gauhati: Western Book Depot, 1982.

Baveja, J.D., *The Land Where the Bamboo Flowers*, Gauhati: Publications Board, Assam, 1970.

Bharali, D. (ed.), *Economic Development of the North-Eastern Region*, Gauhati: Spectrum Publications, 1988.

Bhattacharjee, J.B., *Social Tension in North-East India*, Calcutta: Research India Publications, 1982.

Bhattacharjee, J.B., (ed.), *Sequences of Development in North-East India*, Guwahati: Omsons Publications, 1989.

Bhattacharjee, J.B., *The Garos and the English*, New Delhi: Radiant Publishers, 1978.

Bhattacharjee, P.N., *The Koloi — in the Light of the People's History*, Agartala: Deptt. of Welfare for Scheduled Tribes & Scheduled Castes, Govt. of Tripura, 1983.

Bhattacharjee, P.N., *The Jamatia of Tripura*, Agartala: Deptt. of Welfare for Scheduled Tribes & Scheduled Castes, Govt. of Tripura, 1984.

Bhattacharjee, S.R., *Tribal Insurgency in Tripura*, Delhi: Inter-India Publications, 1989.

Bhattacharjee, T., *Sociology of the Karbis*, Delhi: B.R. Publishing Corp., 1986.

Bhattacharjee, T.K., *The Tangams*, Shillong: Research Department, Government of Arunachal Pradesh, 1975.

Bhattacharjee, T.K., *The Idus of Mathun and Dri Valley*, Shillong: Director of Research, Govt. of Arunachal Pradesh, 1983.

Bhattacharyya, B., *Tripura Administration — The Era of Modernisation*, Delhi: Mittal Publications, 1986.

Borah, J., *Spatial Structure of Urban Influence in the Neighbouring Areas of Gauhati City*, Delhi: Inter-India Publications, 1985.

Bordoloi, B.N., *Chomangkan — The Death Ceremony Performed by the Karbis*, Guwahati: Tribal Research Institute, 1982.

Bordoloi, B.N., *The Dimasa Kacharis of Assam*, Guwahati: Tribal Research Institute, 1976.

Borodoloi, B.N., *United Mikir and North Cachar Hills*, Shillong: Tribal Research Institute, 1972.

Bose, A., T. Nongbri and N. Kumar (eds.), *Tribal Demography and Development in North-East India*, Delhi: B.R. Publishing Corp., 1990.

Bose, M.L., *Social History of Assam*, New Delhi: Concept Publishing Co., 1989.

Bose, J.K., *Glimpses of Tribal Life in North-East India*, Calcutta: Institute of Social Research and Applied Anthropology, 1980.

Cantlie, Audrey, *The Assamese*, London: University, 1984.

Chattopadhayaya, S.K., *The Jaintias*, New Delhi: Cosmo Publications, 1988.

Chattopadhayaya, S.K., *Tribal Institutions of Meghalaya*, Gauhati: Spectrum Publications, 1985.

Chaube, S.K., *Hill Politics in North-East India*, New Delhi: Orient Longman, 1973.

Chaube, S.K., *Electoral Politics in North-East India*, Madras: Universities Press (India) Pvt. Ltd., 1985.

Chaudhuri, T.K., *Demographic Trends in Assam, 1921–71*, Delhi: B.R. Publishing Corp., 1982.

Chauhan, S.K., *Caste, Status and Power* (*Social Stratification in Assam*), New Delhi: Classical Publishing Co., 1980.

Choudhury, J.N., *A Comparative Study of Adi Religion*, Shillong: DIPR, NEFA, 1971.

Choudhury, J.N., *Arunachal Panorama — A Study in Profile*, Shillong: J. Chowdhury, 1973.

Choudhury, J.N., *The Khasi Canvas*, Shillong: J. Chowdhury, 1978.

Choudhury, J.N., *Arunachal Pradesh — From Frontier Tracts to Union Territory*, New Delhi: Cosmo Publications, 1983.

Choudhury, J.N., *The Tribal Culture and History of Arunachal Pradesh*, Delhi: Daya Publishing House, 1990.

Choudhury, M.M., *Tribes of Assam Plains*, Guwahati: Director, Welfare of Plains Tribes & Backward Classes, Assam, 1980.

Constantine, R., *Manipur — Maid of the Mountains*, New Delhi: Lancer Publications, 1981.

Danda, Dipali G., *Among the Dimasa of Assam — An Ethnographic Study*, New Delhi: Sterling Publishers Pvt. Ltd., 1978.

Danda, D.G. & S. Ghatak, *The Semsa and their Habitat*, Calcutta: Anthropological Survey of India, 1985.

Das, B.M. (ed.), Contemporary Anthropological Research in North-East India, in the *Bulletin of the Department of Anthropology*, Dibrugarh: Department of Anthropology, Dibrugarh University, 1974.

Das, B.M., *The People of Assam*, Delhi: Gian Publishing House, 1987.

Das, N.K., *Ethnic Identity, Ethnicity and Social Stratification in North-East India*, Delhi: Inter-India Publications, 1989.

Das, B.K., *Manipur Tribal Scene—Studies in Society & Change*, Delhi: Inter-India Publications, 1985.

Das, S.K., *Spotlight on Assam*, Chanderpur (Maharashtra): Premier Book Service, 1989.

Das, S.T., *Tribal Life of North-East India*, Delhi: Gian Publishing House, 1986.

Das, B., *A Glimpse of the Scheduled Castes and their Socio-Economic Development in Assam*, Guwahati: Omsons Publications, 1986.

Das Gupta, B.K., A. Basu, B. Ray Chaudhuri & P. Gupta (eds.), *Proceedings of the Symposium on Puram (Chote) Revisited*, Calcutta: Anthropological Survey of India, 1985.

Das Gupta, P.K., *Life and Culture of Matrilineal Tribe of Meghalaya*, Delhi: Inter-India Publications, 1984.

Das S.T., *Life-Style — Indian Tribes (Locational Practice)*, Vol. I, Delhi: Gian Publishing House, 1987.

Das R.K., *Tribal Social Structure—A Study of the Maring Society of Manipur*, Delhi: Inter-India Publications, 1988.

Datta, B. & A. Choudhury (eds.), *Modern Assemese Life and Culture*, Guwhati: Assam Academy for Cultural Relations, 1985.

Datta-Ray, B. (ed.), *Social and Economic Profile of North-East India*, Delhi: B.R. Publishing Corp., 1978.

Datta-Ray, B. (ed.), *The Emergence and Role of Middle Class in North-East India*, New Delhi: Uppal Publishing House, 1983.

Datta-Ray, B. (ed.), *The Pattern and Problems of Population in North-East India*, New Delhi: Uppal Publishing House, 1986.

Datta-Ray, B. (ed.), *North-East India — A.D. 2000*, New Delhi: Deep & Deep Publications, 1987.

Datta-Ray, B., *Tribal Identity and Tension in North-East India,* New Delhi: Omsons Publications, 1989.

Datta-Ray, B., D.N. Majumdar & D. Doley (eds.), *Crime Prespective in North-East India,* Guwhati: Omsons Publications, 1986.

Deb Roy, H.L., *A Tribe in Transition—The Jaintias of Meghalaya,* New Delhi: Cosmo Publications, 1980.

Debbarman, D., *Treatise on Traditional Institutions of the Tripuri Community,* Agartala: Deptt. of Welfare for Scheduled Tribes & Scheduled Castes, Govt. of Tripura, 1983.

Department of Sociology, NEHU, *Proceedings of the Seminar on Youth Problem and Movements,* Shillong: Department of Sociology, NEHU, 1978.

Deuri, R.K., *The Sulungs,* Shillong: Director of Research, Government of Arunachal Pradesh, 1982.

Dev, B.J. & D.K. Lahiri, *Cosmology of Caste and Social Mobility in Assam,* Delhi: Mittal Publications, 1984.

Dev, B.J. and D.K. Lahiri, *Manipur — Culture and Politics,* Delhi: Mittal Publications, 1987.

Dev, B.J. & D.K. Lahiri, *Lushai Customs and Ceremonies,* Delhi: Mittal Publications, 1983.

Dhasmana, M.M., *The Ramos of Arunachal — A Socio-Cultural Study,* Delhi: Concept Publishing Co., 1979.

Duarah, D.K., *The Monpas of Arunachal Pradesh,* Itanagar: Director of Research, Govt. of Arunachal Pradesh, 1990.

Dutta, B. (ed.), *Focus on Folklore of North-East India,* Guwahati: Assam Academy for Cultural Relations, 1985.

Dutta, B.B. (ed.), *Land Use Pattern in North-East India,* Ludhiana: Gagan Publications, 1986.

Dutta, P. *The Noctes,* Shillong: DIPR, Government of Arunachal Pradesh, 1978.

Dutta, P. (a), *The Singphos,* Itanagar: Director of Research, Govt. of Arunachal Pradesh, 1990.

Dutta, P. (b), *The Wanchos,* Itanagar: Director of Research, Govt. of Arunachal Pradesh, 1990.

Dutta, P.C. & D.K. Duarah (eds.), *Aspects of Culture and Customs of Arunachal Pradesh,* Itanagar: Director of Research, Govt. of Arunachal Pradesh, 1990.

Dutta, P.N., *Impact of the West on Khasi and Jaintias — A Survey of Political, Economic and Social Change,* New Delhi: Cosmo Publications, 1982.

Dutta, S., *The Mataks and Their Kingdom—Castes and Tribes of Assam,* Allahabad: Chugh Publications, 1985.

Dutta-Goswami, P., *Essays on the Folklore and Culture of North-East India,* Gauhati: Spectrum Publications. 1982.

Gan Choudhri, J., *The Riangs of Tripura,* Agartala: Deptt. of Welfare for Scheduled Tribes & Scheduled Castes, Govt. of Tripura, 1983.

Gan-Chaudhuri, J., *A Corpus of Tripura,* Delhi: Inter-India Publications, 1990.

Ganguli, M., *A Pilgrimage to the Nagas,* New Delhi: Oxford & IBH Publishing Co., 1984.

Gassah, L.S. (ed.), *Garo Hills — Land and the People,* New Delhi: Omsons Publications, 1984.

Ghosh, K., *Tribal Insurrection in Tripura—A Study in Relative Deprivation,* Hyderabad: Booklinks Corp., 1984.

Ghurye, G.S., *The Burning Caldron of North-East India,* Bombay: Popular Prakashan Pvt. Ltd., 1980.

Gogoi, Pradip Kumar, *The Economy of Karbi Anglong,* Gauhati: Directorate of Economics & Statistics, Govt. of Assam, 1978.

Gogoi, P., *Tai-Ahom: Religion and Customs,* Gauhati: Publications Board, Assam, 1976.

Gohain, B.C., *Human Sacrifice and Head-hunting in North-East India,* Gauhati: Lawyer's Book Stall, 1977.

Goswami, B.B. (ed.), *Cultural Profile of Shillong,* Calcutta: Anthropological Survey of India, 1979.

Goswami, H., *Population Trends in the Brahmaputra Valley,* Delhi: Mittal Publications, 1985.

Goswami, M.C. & D.N. Majumdar, *Social Institutions of the Garo of Meghalaya — An Analytical Study,* Calcutta: R. Saha, 1972.

Goswami, P.C., *Socio-Economic Research in Tribal Areas,* Jorhat (Assam): Agro-Economic Research Centre for North-East India, 1971.

Goswami, P.D., *Bohag Bihu of Assam and Bihu Songs,* Guwahati: Publications Board, Assam, 1988.

Goswami, T., *Kuki-Life and Lore,* Vol. I, Haflong (Assam): North Cachar Hills District Council, 1985.

Guha Thakurta, S.N., *Tripura,* New Delhi: National Book Trust, 1986.

Haimendorf, Christoph Von Fürer, *Highlanders of Arunachal Pradesh — Anthropological Research in North-East India,* New Delhi: Vikas Publishing House Pvt. Ltd., 1982.

Harlalka, S.S., *Tea Garden Labourers of Assam,* Dhubri (Assam): People's Publishing House, 1975.

Horam, M., *Nagas: Old Ways New Trends,* Delhi: B.R. Publishing Corp., 1988.

Horam, M., *Social and Cultural Life of the Nagas — The Tangkhul Nagas,* Delhi: B.R. Publishing Corp., 1977.

Jha, S.D. *The Wealth of Arunachal Pradesh,* Delhi: Mittal Publications, 1985.

Jha, S.D., *Socio-Economic and Demographic Dimensions of Arunachal Pradesh,* Guwahati: Omsons Publications, 1988.

Kabui, G., *Anal: A Transborder Tribe of Manipur,* Delhi: Mittal Publications, 1985.

Kar, M., *Muslims in Assam Politics,* Delhi: Omsons Publications, 1990.

Kar, P.C., *The Garos in Transition,* New Delhi: Cosmo Publications, 1982.

Kar-Choudhury, A.B., *Tribal Songs of North-East India,* Calcutta: Firma KLM Pvt. Ltd., 1984.

Karotemprel, S. & B. Datta-Ray (eds.): *Tea-Garden Labourers of North-East India,* Shillong: Vendrame Institute, 1979.

Karotemprel, S., *The Tribes of North-East India,* Shillong: Vendrame Missiological Institute, 1984.

Karotemprel, S., *Albizuri Among the Lyngams (A Brief History of the Catholic Mission Among the Lyngams of North-East India),* Shillong: Vendrame Missiological Institute, 1985.

Khan, W. & K.S. Ramesh, *Integrated Area Development Plan for West District, Manipur,* Hyderabad: National Institute of Community Development, 1976.

Kumar, K., *The Pailibos,* DIPR, Govt. of Arunachal Pradesh, 1979.

Kyndiah, P.R., *Meghalaya — Yesterday and Today,* New Delhi: Vikas Publishing House, 1990.

Lal, P. & B.K. Das Gupta, *Lower Siang People,* Calcutta: Anthropological Survey of India, 1979.

Lalbiakthanga, *The Mizos — A Study in Racial Personality,* Gauhati: United Publishers, 1978.

Luingam, L. and N. Haksar, *Nagaland File — A Question of Human Rights,* New Delhi: Lancer International, 1984.

Majumdar, D.N., *A Study of Culture Changes in Two Garo Villages of Meghalaya,* Gauhati: University of Gauhati, 1980.

Majumdar, D.N., & B. Datta-Ray, *Tribal Occupational Mobility,* Calcutta: Research India Publications, 1984.

Marak, J., *Garo Customary Laws and Practice — A Sociological Study,* Calcutta: Firma KLM Pvt. Ltd., 1986.

Mathew, T. (ed.), *Tribal Economy of North-Eastern Region,* Guwahati: Spectrum Publications, 1980.

Mathur, P.R.G., *Khasi of Meghalaya — Study in Tribalism & Religion,* New Delhi: Cosmo Publications, 1979.

Mawrie, H.O. & Sujata Miri (eds.), *The Khasi Milieu,* Delhi: Concept Publishing Co., 1981.

Miri, M. (ed.), *Linguistic Situation in North-East India,* Shillong: North-Eastern Council for Social Sciences Research, 1982.

Miri, S. (ed.), *Religion and Society of North-East India,* New Delhi: Vikas Publishing House Pvt. Ltd., 1980.

Nag, S., *Roots of Ethnic Conflict (Nationality Question in North-East India),* New Delhi: Manohar Publications, 1990.

Nair, M.K.S., *Tribal Economy in Transition,* Delhi: Inter-India Publications, 1987.

Nair, P.T., *Tribes of Arunachal Pradesh,* Gauhati: Spectrum Publications, 1985.

Nanda, N., *The Land of Mon,* New Delhi: Vikas Publishing House Pvt. Ltd., 1982.

Natrajan, N., *The Missionary Among the Khasis,* New Delhi: Sterling Publishers Pvt. Ltd., 1977.

National Institute of Public Cooperation and Child Development, *Report of the Seminar on Tribal Situation in North-East India,* Guwahati, 1982.

Neog, M., *Tradition and Style.* Jorhat (Assam): Assam Sahitya Sabha, 1981.

NERC-ICSSR, *Proceedings of the Seminar on the Status of Women in Naga Societies,* Shillong, 1988.

NERC-ICSSR, *Proceedings of the Seminar on the Status of Women in Tribal Cultures of Meghalaya,* Shillong, 1988.

NERC-ICSSR, *Proceedings of the Seminar on the Status of Women in Non-Tribal Societies of Assam,* Dibrugarh, 1988.

NERC-ICSSR, *Proceedings of the Seminar on the Status of Women in Tribal Societies of Mizoram,* Aizawl, 1988.

North-Eastern Institute of Anthropological Research, *Proceedings of the Seminar on the Status of Women in Barak Valley,* Silchar, 1988.

NERC-ICSSR, *Proceedings of the Seminar on Sociology of Resource Use with special reference to Mizoram,* Lunglei (Mizoram), 1990.

Pakem, B. (ed.), *Shillong 1971–81,* Calcutta: Research India Publications, 1984.

Pakam, B. (ed.), *Nationality, Ethnicity and Cultural Identity in North-East India,* Guwahati: Omsons Publications, 1990.

Panchani, C.S., *Manipur: Religion, Culture and Society,* New Delhi: Konark Publishers Pvt. Ltd., 1987.

Panchani, C.S., *Arunachal Pradesh: Religion, Culture and Society,* New Delhi: Konark Publishers Pvt. Ltd., 1989.

Pandey, B.B., *The Hill Miri,* Shillong: DIPR, Govt. of Arunachal Pradesh, 1974.

Parratt, S.N., *The Religion of Manipur,* Calcutta: Firma KLM, 1980.

Paul, M.C., *Dimensions of Tribal Movements in India — A Study of Udayachal in Assam Valley,* Delhi: Inter-India Publications, 1989.

Payeng, H., *Economic and Social Change in North-East,* New Delhi: Criterion Publications, 1988.

Pegu, N.C., *The Mishings of the Brahmaputra Valley,* Dhamaji (Assam): Mrs. M. Pegu, 1981.

Phukan, U., *The Ex-Tea Garden Labour Population in Assam,* Delhi: B.R. Publishing Corp., 1984.

Prakash Singh, *India — The Land and People* (*Nagaland*), New Delhi: National Book Trust, 1972.

Rajguru, S., *Medieval Assamese Society,* Nagaon (Assam): Asami, 1988.

Ramunny, M., *The World of Nagas,* New Delhi: Northern Book Centre, 1988.

Rana, B.S. (Capt.), *The People of Meghalaya—Study on the People and their Religio-Cultural Life*, Calcutta: Punthi Pustak, 1989.

Rao, V.V., *A Century of Tribal Politics in North-East India (1874–1974)*, New Delhi: S. Chand & Co., 1976.

Roy, R. Kostan, *Assortment from Tribal Research Institute, Meghalaya*, Shillong: Tribal Research Institute, 1978.

Roy, S. & S.H.N. Rizvi, *Tribal Customary Laws of North-East India*, Delhi: B.R. Publishing Corp., 1990.

Roy-Burman, B.K., *Towards Poverty Alleviation Programmes in Nagaland and Manipur*, Delhi: Mittal Publications, 1983.

Roychoudhury, P., *The North-East: Roots of Insurgency*, Calcutta: Firma KLM Publications, 1986.

Saha, S.B. (a), *Tribes of Tripura—A Historical Survey*, Agartala; Siddharta Saha, 1986.

Saha, S.B. (b), *Socio-Economic Survey of the Noatia Tribes*, Agartala: Tribal Welfare Department, Govt. of Tripura, 1986.

Saigal, Omesh, *Tripura — Its History and Culture*, Delhi: Concept Publishing Co., 1978.

Saikia, N. (ed.), *Assam and the Assamese Mind*, Gauhati: Assam Sahitya Sabha, 1980.

Saikia, P.C., *The Dibongiyas*, Delhi: B.R. Publishing Corp., 1976.

Saikia, P.D. & U. Phukan, *Rural Development in North-East India*, Delhi: B.R. Publishing Corp., 1989.

Sanajnoba, N., *Manipur — Past and Present*, Vol. I, Delhi: Mittal Publications, 1988.

Sangma, M.S., *History and Culture of the Garos*, New Delhi: Books Today, 1981.

Sarkar, J. & B. Datta Ray (eds.), *Social and Political Institutions of the Hill People of North-East India*, Calcutta: Anthropological Survey of India, 1990.

Sarma, R.M., *A Political History of Tripura*, Calcutta: Puthipatra, 1986.

Sarma, S., *A Socio-Economic and Cultural History of Medieval Assam (1200–1800 AD)*, Guwahati: Pratima Devi, 1989.

Sen, S., *The Tribes of Meghalaya — A Bibliography*, Delhi: Mittal Publications, 1985.

Sen, S., *Arunachal Pradesh and the Tribes — A Select Bibliography*, Delhi: Gian Publishing House, 1986.

Sen, S., *Tribes of Nagaland,* Delhi: Mittal Publications, 1987.

Sen, S., *Social and State Formation in Khasi Jaintia Hills,* Delhi: B.R. Publishing Corp., 1985.

Shadap-Sen, N.C., *The Origin and Early History of the Khasi-Synteng People,* Calcutta: Firma KLM, 1981.

Sharma, M., *Social and Economic Change in Assam — Middle Class Hegemony,* Delhi: Ajanta Publications, 1990.

Sharma, T.C. & D.N. Majumdar (eds.), *Eastern Himalayas — A Study on Anthropology and Tribalism,* New Delhi: Cosmo Publications, 1980.

Sharma-Thakur, G.C., *The Tai Phakes of Assam,* Delhi: B.R. Publishing Corp., 1982.

Sharma-Thakur, G.C., *The Lalungs (Tiwas),* Guwahati: Tribal Research Institute, 1985.

Singh, B., *Politics of Alienation in Assam,* Delhi: Ajanta Publications, 1984.

Singh, J.P., *Urban Land Use Planning in Hill Areas: A Case Study of Shillong,* Delhi: Inter-India Publications, 1980.

Singh, J.P., *Human Resources of North-Eastern India,* Delhi: Inter-India Publications, 1982.

Sinha, R., *Religion and Culture of North-East India,* New Delhi: Abhinav Publications, 1977.

Singh, R. (Capt.), *The Anals of Manipur,* Imphal: Director for Social Welfare of Tribals and Backward Classes, Govt. of Manipur, 1981.

Srivastava, L.R.N., *Among the Wanchos,* Shillong: DIPR, Govt. of Arunachal Pradesh, 1973.

Srivastava, L.R.N., *Social Organization of the Minyongs,* Itanagar: Director of Research, Govt. of Arunachal Pradesh, 1990.

Srivastava, S.C., *Demographic Profile of North-East India,* Delhi: Mittal Publications, 1987.

Terwiel, B.J., *The Tai of Assam and Ancient Tai Ritual — Life Cycle Ceremonies,* Vol. I, Gaya (Bihar): The South-East Asian Review Office, 1980.

Terwiel, B.J., *The Tai of Assam and Ancient Tai Ritual — Sacrifices and Time Reckoning,* Vol. II, Gaya (Bihar): The South-East Asian Review Office, 1981.

Vidyarthi, L.P., *Art and Culture of North-East India,* New Delhi: Publications Division, Min. of I & B, GOI, 1986.